THE BEATITU
6 STUDIES FOR GROUP!

CW00689666

# SHOWING MERCY

*Getting What You Give*

# David Lambert

ZondervanPublishingHouse
*Grand Rapids, Michigan*

*A Division of* HarperCollins*Publishers*

SHOWING MERCY: GETTING WHAT YOU GIVE
Copyright © 1993 by David Lambert
All rights reserved

Requests for information should be addressed to:
Zondervan Publishing House
Grand Rapids, MI 49530

ISBN 0-310-59663-7

*Edited by Jack Kuhatschek*
*Cover design by John M. Lucas*
*Cover photograph by Mike Carter*
*Interior design by Louise Bauer*

*Printed in the United States of America*

93  94  95  96  97  98 / ❖ DP / 10  9  8  7  6  5  4  3  2  1

# Contents

# The Beatitude Series

Welcome to the Beatitude Series. This series is designed to help you develop the eight character qualities found in those whom Jesus calls "blessed."

The Beatitudes are among the best-known and best-loved words of Jesus. They form the heart of the Sermon on the Mount, found in Matthew 5–7 and Luke 6:17–49. In eight brief statements Jesus describes the lifestyle that God desires and rewards:

> *Blessed are the poor in spirit,*
> *  for theirs is the kingdom of heaven.*
> *Blessed are those who mourn,*
> *  for they will be comforted.*
> *Blessed are the meek,*
> *  for they will inherit the earth.*

*Blessed are those who hunger and thirst for righteousness,*
*    for they will be filled.*
*Blessed are the merciful,*
*    for they will be shown mercy.*
*Blessed are the pure in heart,*
*    for they will see God.*
*Blessed are the peacemakers,*
*    for they will be called sons of God.*
*Blessed are those who are persecuted because of righteousness,*
*    for theirs is the kingdom of heaven.*

The Beatitudes turn the world's values upside down. We are tempted to say: "*Wretched* are the poor, for they have so little money. *Wretched* are those who mourn, for no one will hear their cries. *Wretched* are the meek, for they will be trampled by the powerful." Yet Jesus shatters our stereotypes and asserts that the poor will be rich, the mourners will be comforted, and the meek will inherit everything. What a strange kingdom he offers!

In recent years there has been some confusion about the kind of blessing Christ promises in these verses. The Beatitudes have been described as "God's prescription for happiness." One book has even called them "The Be-Happy Attitudes."

The Greek word *makarios* can mean "happy." J. B. Phillips translates the opening words of each beatitude, "How happy are . . . !" Nevertheless, John Stott writes:

> It is seriously misleading to render *makarios* "happy." For happiness is a subjective state, whereas Jesus is making an objective judgment about these people. He is declaring not what they may feel like ("happy"), but what God thinks of them and what on that account they are: they are "blessed."[1]

The eight guides in the Beatitude Series give you an in-depth look at each beatitude. But Jesus is not describing eight different types of people—some who are meek, others who are merciful, and still others who are peacemakers. He desires to see all eight character qualities in every one of his followers.

That's a tall order! Only those who enter Christ's kingdom by faith can expect such a transformation. And only those who serve the King can enjoy his rewards.

Our prayer is that The Beatitude Series will give you a clearer and deeper grasp of what it truly means to be blessed.

## HOW TO USE THE BEATITUDE SERIES

The Beatitude Series is designed to be flexible. You can use the guides in any order that is best for you or your group. They are ideal for Sunday-school classes, small groups, one-on-one relationships, or as materials for your quiet times.

Because each guide contains only six studies, you can easily explore more than one beatitude. In a Sunday-school class, any two guides can be combined for a quarter (twelve weeks), or the entire series can be covered in a year.

Each study deliberately focuses on a limited number of passages, usually only one or two. That allows you to see each passage in its context, avoiding the temptation of prooftexting and the frustration of "Bible hopscotch" (jumping from verse to verse). If you would like to look up additional passages, a Bible concordance will give the most help.

The Beatitude Series helps you *discover* what the Bible says rather than simply *telling* you the answers. The questions encourage you to think and to explore options rather than merely to fill in the blanks with one-word answers.

Leader's notes are provided in the back of each guide. They show how to lead a group discussion, provide additional information on questions, and suggest ways to deal with problems that may come up in the discussion. With such helps, someone with little or no experience can lead an effective study.

## SUGGESTIONS FOR INDIVIDUAL STUDY

1. Begin each study with prayer. Ask God to help you understand the passage and to apply it to your life.

2. A good modern translation, such as the *New International Version,* the *New American Standard Bible,* or the *New Revised Standard Version,* will give you the most help. Questions in this guide, however, are based on the *New International Version.*

3. Read and reread the passage(s). You must know what the passage says before you can understand what it means and how it applies to you.

4. Write your answers in the space provided in the study guide. This will help you to clearly express your understanding of the passage.

5. Keep a Bible dictionary handy. Use it to look up any unfamiliar words, names, or places.

## SUGGESTIONS FOR GROUP STUDY

1. Come to the study prepared. Careful preparation will greatly enrich your time in group discussion.

2. Be willing to join in the discussion. The leader of the group will not be lecturing but will encourage people to discuss what they have learned in the passage. Plan to share what God has taught you in your individual study.

3. Stick to the passage being studied. Base your answers on the verses being discussed rather than on outside authorities such as commentaries or your favorite author or speaker.

4. Try to be sensitive to the other members of the group. Listen attentively when they speak, and be affirming whenever you can. This will encourage more hesitant members of the group to participate.

**5.** Be careful not to dominate the discussion. By all means participate! But allow others to have equal time.

**6.** If you are the discussion leader, you will find additional suggestions and helpful ideas in the leader's notes at the back of the guide.

## Note

1. *The Message of the Sermon on the Mount* (Downers Grove, Ill.: InterVarsity Press, 1978), p. 33.

# *Introducing Showing Mercy*

> *Blessed are the merciful,*
> *for they will be shown mercy.*

In Victor Hugo's classic *Les Misérables,* Jean Valjean, newly released from prison, is unable to find food or lodging because of the distrust and hatred of the people. Finally, he knocks on the door of a kindly bishop.

"Look. My name is Jean Valjean. I'm a convict on parole. I've done nineteen years in prison. They let me out four days ago. . . . I'm ready to pay, I don't care how much, I've got the money. I'm very tired, twelve leagues on foot, and I'm hungry. Will you let me stay?"

"Mme Magliore," says the bishop, "will you please lay another place [at the table]."[1]

But despite the bishop's kindness, Valjean steals the bishop's valuable silverware during the night and escapes out a window.

When the French police routinely question Valjean, discover the silver, and haul him back to the cathedral, the kind bishop greets him enthusiastically: "So here you are! . . . I'm delighted to see you. Had you forgotten that I gave you the candlesticks as well? They're silver like the rest, and worth a good two hundred francs."[2]

The bishop then dismisses the puzzled policemen, places the candlesticks in Valjean's bag, and says quietly, "Do not . . . ever forget that you have promised me to use the money to make yourself an honest man."[3]

Within twenty-four hours, Valjean finds himself on his knees, converted both to the Christian faith and to a lifestyle of honesty.

Mercy, such as that evidenced by Hugo's bishop, has great power in people's lives. Like many of the other attitudes and qualities Christ commended in the beatitudes—meekness, spiritual poverty, a pure heart—mercy is deceptive; it is often interpreted as weakness rather than strength. Yet this weakness has power to change lives.

John Stott defines mercy as "compassion for people in need."[4] *The Expositor's Bible Commentary* explains that "mercy embraces both forgiveness for the guilty and compassion for the suffering and needy."[5] In his exposition of the Sermon on the Mount, James Montgomery Boice writes that "mercy is love reaching out to help those who are helpless and who need salvation. Mercy identifies with the miserable in their misery."[6]

Mercy is both a royal and a divine attribute, as Shakespeare points out in *The Merchant of Venice:*

> The quality of mercy is not strained,
> It droppeth as the gentle rain from heaven
> Upon the place beneath. It is twice blest;
> It blesseth him that gives and him that takes.
> 'Tis mightiest in the mightiest. It becomes
> The throned monarch better than his crown.
> It is an attribute to God himself,
> And earthly power doth then show likest God's
> When mercy seasons justice. Therefore, . . .

Though justice be thy plea, consider this,
That in the course of justice none of us
Should see salvation. We do pray for mercy,
And that same prayer doth teach us all to render
The deeds of mercy.[7]

For the Christian, mercy is not an option—it is a necessity. We rely on God's mercy, as Shakespeare pointed out, for our salvation. We are to "be merciful, just as [our] Father is merciful." If we want to receive mercy, we must be willing to give it. And we are told that God does not demand that we follow pharisaical rules and laws, but rather desires mercy, justice, and humble fellowship with him.

"Blessed are the merciful," indeed.

May you be convinced as you participate in this study, as I was while I worked on it, that our hearts must be filled with mercy if we are to please the merciful God we serve.

*David Lambert*

## Notes

1. *Les Misérables* (New York: Penguin Books, 1982), pp. 84–85.
2. Ibid, pp. 110–11.
3. Ibid, p. 111.
4. John Stott, *The Message of the Sermon on the Mount*, p. 47.
5. Frank E. Gaebelein, gen. ed., *The Expositor's Bible Commentary, Volume 8* (Grand Rapids: Zondervan Publishing House, 1984), p. 134.
6. James Montgomery Boice, *The Sermon on the Mount* (Grand Rapids: Zondervan Publishing House, 1972), p. 51.
7. G. B. Harrison, ed., *Shakespeare: The Complete Works* (New York: Harcourt, Brace & World, Inc., 1968), p. 606.

# God's Great Mercy to Us

*ROMANS 3:9–20; EPHESIANS 2:1–10*

In April of 1991, Jermaine Washington, a 23-year-old man in Washington, D.C., donated a kidney to his friend Michelle Stevens. Michelle's older brother had at first offered to donate one, but then changed his mind, afraid of the weeks of pain that would result. Michelle's boyfriend gave her two diamond rings as a token of his love, but giving her a kidney was going too far. Jermaine accepted the pain as the price for helping his friend.

Without Jermaine's kidney, Michelle would soon have died. Her friend's merciful gift brought her from the brink of physical death to physical life.

God's mercy, similarly, is the difference between spiritual death and spiritual life for us all. The passages in this study demonstrate just how great an act of mercy that is.

1. All of us have habits or character traits we wish we could change. What are some things you wish you could change about yourself?

**2.** Read Romans 3:9–20. One of the ways points are emphasized in Scripture is through repetition. In Romans 3:10–18, what are some points God doesn't want you to miss?

**3.** How does each body part Paul mentions (throat, tongue, lips, mouth, feet, eyes) illustrate the impact sin had on our lives (vv. 13–18)?

**4.** Verses 13 and 14 talk about sins of the "lips" and "tongue." What "mouth" sins can Christians sometimes be guilty of—perhaps without realizing it?

**5.** What does Paul conclude about those who are measured against the standard of God's law (vv. 19–20)?

**6.** Read Ephesians 2:1–9. How does Paul describe our lifestyle as non-Christians (vv. 1–3)?

**7.** Verses 1 and 5 talk about being "dead" in transgressions. In what ways can a sinful person be described as "dead"?

**8.** How does the depth of your sin help you to realize God's great love for you, his rich mercy, and the incomparable riches of his grace (vv. 4, 7)?

In what ways have you seen those attributes of God operate in your life?

**9.** What does it mean that God has made us "alive" in Christ (v. 5)?

**10.** What can spiritually "alive" people do that spiritually "dead" people can't?

**11.** Why does Paul also emphasize that we have been "raised up with Christ" and "seated with him in the heavenly realms" (vv. 6–7)?

**12.** What images come to mind when you think of God lavishing his grace and kindness on you throughout the coming ages (v. 7)?

**13.** How would you paraphrase verses 8 and 9 so that their meaning would be clear to someone who has never heard them before?

**14.** Why is God's great mercy to us the foundation for our showing mercy to others?

**MEMORY VERSE**

*But because of his great love for us, God, who is rich in mercy, made us alive with Christ even when we were dead in transgressions—it is by grace you have been saved.*

Ephesians 2:4–5

## BETWEEN STUDIES

In your answer to question 10, you identified several things that being "alive in Christ" makes possible for you. Perhaps you identified an ability to love the unlovely, or to present your prayers to God in confidence that he loves you and that he will listen, or to receive instruction and guidance from the Holy Spirit. Review those items now and decide in practical terms what those items actually mean in your daily life. Concentrate in the coming week on appropriating and enjoying your "aliveness" in Christ as fully as possible, being aware each day of that wonderful privilege.

## FOR FURTHER STUDY

It is impossible to understand God's mercy without understanding how short we fall of deserving his love. The verses in Romans 3:10–18 are actually quotations of Old Testament passages. Review those passages—some of which will be familiar to you—for a better grasp of how wicked we appear in God's sight: Psalm 14:1–6; Ecclesiastes 7:20; Psalms 5:8–10; 10:2–11; 140:1–3; 59:5–9; 36:1–4. Contrast the hopeless tone of these verses with the positive tone of Romans 6:1–10, where Paul expands his discussion of being made "alive in Christ."

# 2

# Being Merciful to Others

*LUKE 6:32–36;*
*MATTHEW 5:43–6:4*

Several years ago, I was asked to speak to a group of Christian businessmen. I chose as my text a passage that had become a favorite of mine: Matthew 5, from the Sermon on the Mount.

What a response I got! Even as I was reading the text, before I'd begun to speak about it, the men began to shake their heads at each other, frown, and snicker. One lawyer leaned toward his partner and said in a stage-whisper, "We'd be out of business!"

And well they might—if, instead of suing their enemies, they loved them. The men around those tables tried to live by sound business practices: outsmarting your competitors, staying one step ahead of them, taking advantage of their weaknesses. But Christ preaches a different gospel in the Sermon on the Mount, a gospel of mercy and love, a gospel of turning the other cheek and going the extra mile. In the passages in this study, we begin to see just how costly a virtue mercy can be.

1. The Golden Rule ("Do unto others as you would have them do unto you") doesn't seem to be the dominant ethic of our society. How could that Golden Rule be re-phrased to reflect how most people in our culture *really* treat others?

2. Read Luke 6:32–36. What standards does God set for "sinners" and "saints" in verses 32–35?

3. Think of someone in your life who loved you and was kind to you even when you didn't (or couldn't) recipro-cate. How did that person's love affect you?

   How do you remember that person now?

**4.** How might Christ's standard of unconditional love and mercy be acted out:

❑ In marriage?

❑ In parenting?

❑ In the workplace?

❑ In friendships?

**5.** What incidents from Jesus' life illustrate this principle of merciful behavior to those who neither deserved nor returned it?

**6.** Read Matthew 5:43–6:4. In what ways should our treatment of others go beyond the standards of society (vv. 43–47)? Why?

**7.** Matthew 5:44 uses the word *enemy*, a word that we define pretty narrowly today. How can we define *enemy* so
that this verse has broader application in our lives, as
Jesus no doubt meant it to?

**8.** Christ warns us about the danger of performing "acts of
righteousness" only to be seen by men (6:1–4). What
safeguards could you practice to make it harder to perform acts of righteousness for the wrong reasons?

**9.** If you gave $100 to a needy person simply so that people
would think you were generous, rather than as an act of
mercy and compassion, what difference would it make to
the one who received the $100? Explain.

What difference would it make to God? to you?

**10.** How might you rewrite the "Golden Rule" to reflect the principles of merciful, godly behavior found in these passages?

## MEMORY VERSE

*Love your enemies, do good to them, and lend to them without expecting to get anything back. Then your reward will be great, and you will be sons of the Most High, because he is kind to the ungrateful and wicked.*

Luke 6:35

## BETWEEN STUDIES

The biblical idea of mercy is hard for us to grasp—and even harder to put into practice. It's best appropriated in doses. This week, try to behave consistently with Luke 6:35: "Love your enemies, do good to them," and Matthew 5:44: "Pray for those who persecute you."

Pick one person in particular who seems to dislike you or to "have it in" for you; pray for that person daily and make every effort to treat that person well and courteously, regardless of how he or she treats you.

When you evaluate your success at the end of the week, don't base your evaluation on any change in that person's attitude, because he or she may decide not to change at all. Base it instead on your own decision to obey Scripture, and what change that obedience brings about in your spiritual life.

## FOR FURTHER STUDY

Read the entire Sermon on the Mount (Matt. 5–7). Make a list of the attitudes and actions Christ encourages in that message that differ from the dominant attitudes and actions of our society.

# Models of Mercy

*MARK 10:46–52; LUKE 10:25–37*

It has become almost synonymous with *mercy.*

Go out of your way to perform a merciful act, and people call you a "Good Samaritan."

There's even a service organization called The Good Samaritans.

Yet in biblical times "Samaritan" was a derogatory term, because the Samaritans, racially and religiously, were a mongrel people—half Jew and half not.

As we look for good role models to follow in our own exercise of mercy, the Bible offers us both the Good Samaritan and the one who created the tale of the Good Samaritan—Jesus, whose exercise of compassion and mercy serves as the ultimate example for us all.

1. Can you think of a time when you expected punishment and instead got a reprieve or forgiveness? How did you feel?

**2.** Read Mark 10:46–52. When Bartimaeus begins to shout, why do you think many rebuke him and tell him to be quiet (v. 48)?

Why do you think Jesus responds differently?

**3.** How does the attitude of the others change as soon as Jesus takes notice of the blind man (v. 49)?

**4.** Although Bartimaeus's ultimate aim is to receive his sight, what is the first thing he requests of Jesus (v. 47)? Why?

**5.** What is Bartimaeus's immediate response when Jesus gives him his sight (v. 52)?

What does this tell us about the ultimate purpose of our merciful acts?

6. Read Luke 10:25–37. What thoughts do you suppose were going through the minds of the priest and the Levite when they saw the injured man?

7. Did the priest and the Levite actually commit any sins in this passage? If so, what?

Why do we think of them so negatively as we read this story?

8. In what practical ways does the Samaritan show mercy to the injured man (vv. 33–35)?

**9.** The Samaritans were hated by the Jews. What groups are similarly unpopular in your community? Why?

**10.** If someone from one of those unpopular groups needed help, would you help? Explain.

If you needed help, and someone from one of those unpopular groups offered it, would you accept?

**11.** Jesus offered the story of the Good Samaritan in response to the law expert's question, "Who is my neighbor?" Based on the parable, what definition of *neighbor* can you give?

## MEMORY VERSE

*"Which of these three do you think was a neighbor to the man who fell into the hands of robbers?" The expert in the law replied, "The one who had mercy on him." Jesus told him, "Go and do likewise."*

Luke 10:36–37

## BETWEEN STUDIES

Almost anyone would have stopped to help a friend or even an acquaintance injured by robbers, but how many of us, like the Samaritan, would have stopped to help a stranger?

This week, watch for opportunities to be of significant help to someone you don't know. Regard this as an important opportunity, something that may be a life-changing event in the life of the person you're helping, and that also may set a new pattern of behavior for you.

## FOR FURTHER STUDY

Nearly all of Jesus' recorded miracles are acts of mercy and compassion. Examine the following passages detailing other acts of compassion by Christ and see what models for your own compassion they provide:

- ❏ Matthew 8:1–4, 14–17; 9:35–38; 14:13–21; 15:29–37; 18:11–13; 20:29–34
- ❏ Mark 9:35–37
- ❏ Luke 7:11–16
- ❏ John 10:11, 14, 15; 11:17–44
- ❏ 2 Corinthians 8:8, 9.

# 4

# Getting What You Give

## MATTHEW 5:7; 18:21–35

In Charles Dickens's ever-popular *A Christmas Carol,* Ebenezer Scrooge begs for mercy when he sees the end to which he is headed, and mercy is granted; he is given another chance. Joyfully, he sets out on Christmas morning to make amends for all the unmerciful acts of which he has been guilty. He starts with the famous prize turkey for the Cratchits, and then proceeds to mend relationships with his niece and nephew, and to give abundantly to charity to make up for "back payments." He even gives Bob Cratchit a raise for his hard work and loyalty over many difficult years.

Old Scrooge understood well—if late—that there is a firm relationship between mercy received and mercy given. And that idea did not originate with Charles Dickens; it is biblical. Showing mercy benefits the merciful one as much as it benefits the recipient, if not more. For as this study will demonstrate, the merciful shall themselves receive mercy.

1. Parents get tired of hearing from their kids, "That's not fair!" when what is meant is that the child didn't get his

way. How would you define *fairness* as it relates to relationships between people?

2. Read Matthew 5:7. Do you think Jesus means that the merciful will be shown mercy by other people, by God, or by both? Explain.

3. Does this verse imply that those who do not extend mercy toward others will *not* receive mercy? If so, what are the implications?

4. Read Matthew 18:21–35. What do you think prompted Peter's question in verse 21?

   How do you suppose he felt about Jesus' answer in verse 22?

**5.** It seems unlikely that Jesus means we are to forgive someone seventy-seven times and no more (v. 22). What point
is he really trying to make?

**6.** The master's proposed action in verse 25—selling the
debtor and his family and all that they owned—seems
cruel to our ears, but at the time it was both legal and ac-
ceptable (see Lev. 25:39; 2 Kings 4:1). What might a com-
parable action be today?

**7.** The amount of money owed in verse 24 is an enormous
sum—millions of dollars. Imagine that you owed someone millions of dollars. How would you repay it?

What effect would that debt have on the quality of your
life for years to come? (Think of your business or liveli-
hood, your credit rating, your spouse, your children's
future, and your leisure time.)

**8.** What is remarkable about the master's response to his servant in verse 27?

How would you feel if your debt of millions of dollars were simply canceled?

**9.** The wicked servant has his debtor "thrown into prison until he could pay the debt" (v. 30). In light of his own experience, why is the servant's action totally inappropriate?

**10.** Clearly this parable is analogous to God's forgiveness of our debt of sin (see v. 35). How would you explain the meaning of this parable with God as the master and us as his servants?

**11.** You began this study by defining *fairness* as it relates to relationships between people. How might you expand your original definition in light of this parable?

## MEMORY VERSE

*Then Peter came to Jesus and asked, "Lord, how many times shall I forgive my brother when he sins against me? Up to seven times?" Jesus answered, "I tell you, not seven times, but seventy-seven times."*

Matthew 18:21–22

## BETWEEN STUDIES

Read James 2:12–13. In your prayer times this week, ask God to remind you of times in the past year when you've shown judgment without mercy. Ask God's forgiveness for not acting in accord with his Word. Then, if any of those to whom you should have shown mercy (and they may be family members) are still available to you, contact them, discuss the incident, and ask their forgiveness for your lack of mercy.

Difficult, isn't it? We tend to concentrate on the way we were wronged or on the justice or "fairness" of our actions. But judgment can be just and still not merciful. Communicating undeserved mercy is truly a Christlike action.

## FOR FURTHER STUDY

Read the parable of the sheep and the goats in Matthew 25:31–46 and compare it with the story of the Good Samaritan in Luke 10:25–37. How does the parable of the sheep and the goats take the parable of the Good Samaritan one step further? Are the priest, the Levite, and the Samaritan sheep or goats? What light does 1 John 3:14–17 shed on God's seemingly harsh judgment in Matthew 25:41–46?

# 5

# Mercy, Not Sacrifice

## MICAH 6:6–8; MATTHEW 12:1–13; 23:23

First Jim Bakker and his associates at PTL, then Jimmy Swaggart and a host of other pastors and evangelists—in recent years, we Christians have witnessed the moral failure of one public Christian figure after another. And we dread the effect those failures must be having on the public's perceptions of Christianity. A recent poll confirmed our fears: Respondents ranked TV evangelists in the *bottom* ten professions for trustworthiness—*below* used-car salesmen.

Before their fall, whether sexual or financial, these individuals had all been very *public* Christians. Outwardly, they went through all the right motions. Like the Pharisee in Luke 18:9–14, they stood in a prominent place and prayed loudly and publicly. Yet they also fell into dishonesty, infidelity, and greed.

Is it possible that they didn't adequately understand the difference between outward religion for appearances and the true religion that pleases God? What, exactly, does God desire of us? The passages we'll look at in this study help answer that question.

1. All of us, at one time or another, have thought of some-one, "What a hypocrite!" When have you felt that about someone, and why? (No names, please.)

2. Read Micah 6:6–8. These verses speak of outward ex-pressions of religion—"burnt offerings," "rivers of oil," and so on—that we no longer practice. What outward signs of religion do we practice today?

3. Is it wrong to practice those outward signs (See Matt. 23:23)? Explain.

   If it isn't wrong, then why does this passage seem to be contrasting those practices with "what is good" (v. 8)?

4. In what ways do we sometimes encourage a "skin-deep" Christianity in each other by reinforcing the outward signs rather than the things the Lord requires of us in verse 8?

**5.** Would it be possible to obey just *half* of God's command in verse 8—for instance, to attempt to walk humbly with God but refuse to act toward others with justice and mercy? Why?

**6.** God doesn't just ask us to *show* mercy; he asks us to *love* mercy. What is the difference?

How could that difference affect the way we live?

**7.** Why is it difficult to act toward others with *both* justice and mercy?

In what ways might we increase our ability to balance these two?

**8.** Read Matthew 12:1–13. Why do you think the Pharisees focus on what is lawful or unlawful rather than on the disciples' hunger or the man's suffering?

**9.** Since there are no actual blood sacrifices discussed in this text, it seems odd that Jesus quotes the Old Testament passage, "I desire mercy, not sacrifice" (v. 7). What types of things is he including under the word *sacrifice*?

**10.** Why would the Pharisees be more likely to show mercy to one of their own sheep than to the man with the shriveled arm (vv. 11–12)?

**11.** What did Jesus do or say in this passage that was so threatening to the Pharisees that they plotted to kill him?

**12.** Read Matthew 23:23. Jesus is clearly saying that some aspects of our spiritual walk are more important than others. How are we to discern the more important aspects?

What principles in these three passages help us in that discernment?

## MEMORY VERSE

*And what does the L*ORD *require of you? To act justly and to love mercy and to walk humbly with your God.*

Micah 6:8

## BETWEEN STUDIES

This week, each time you participate in any religious activity (daily devotions, prayer, church attendance, serving as deacon or usher, witnessing, even saying grace before meals), ask yourself these questions:

- ❏ In what way am I doing this for the Lord and not for myself?
- ❏ In what way am I exercising justice or mercy or walking humbly with God?

If you're not satisfied with your answers, decide what changes in your practices might better express "what is good."

**FOR FURTHER STUDY**

Both Old and New Testaments record instances of people who worshiped according to the letter of the law but whose worship was dishonoring to God because their hearts were proud. Examine 1 Samuel 15:1–26, Isaiah 1:10–20 and 58:3–9, Jeremiah 22:3, and Luke 18:9–14. Now read Matthew 23:12–28, Christ's stinging indictment of hypocrisy.

# 6

# *Responding to God's Mercy*

*HEBREWS 4:14–16;*
*ROMANS 12:1–2*

Meeting with a group of fellow parents, my wife and I discovered that nearly all of us share a common problem: Many of our parenting decisions are motivated by guilt. "We've failed our children!" parents cry. "They're suffering for our mistakes!" And that's often true. But our guilt causes us to compound the problem by making unwise parenting decisions: smothering our children with suffocating love, being too permissive, or spoiling them.

Parents and children would both be better off if we could accept God's forgiveness for our past mistakes. Others we have hurt might not forgive us, but God's mercy is great. And because of his mercy, we can live without guilt, without self-hatred, and without compounding our mistakes. It makes for better parenting—and for better living on all fronts. All of us, not just parents, need God's mercy.

In this study, we'll explore how to receive that mercy, and how to respond to it.

1. Which of the following images is most similar to the way you think of God? Explain why.

   ❏ A distant head of government

   ❏ A benevolent grandfather

   ❏ A therapist

   ❏ A teacher or preacher

   ❏ The neighborhood bully

2. Read Hebrews 4:14–16. Does the description of Christ as one who is able to "sympathize with our weaknesses" (v. 15) match or contradict the image you chose in question 1? Explain.

3. Verse 15 says that Jesus has been tempted "in every way, just as we are." Recall some of the times of significant temptation for you in the past year. Can you imagine Jesus being tempted in those areas? Why or why not?

   What are some of the ways we know from Scripture that Jesus was tempted?

**4.** What are the two things verses 14 and 16 encourage us to do in light of who Jesus is?

How, in practical terms, can we actually do these things?

**5.** Christians generally interpret the phrase "approach the throne of grace" as prayer. Express, in your own words, a prayer that would be effective in helping you to "receive mercy and find grace."

**6.** How does God's mercy actually manifest itself in your life—through physical evidence, emotional evidence, spiritual evidence, social evidence—or what?

**7.** According to verse 16, God provides mercy and grace "to help us in our time of need." At what times are you most in need of mercy and grace?

**8.** Many Christians dislike "foxhole prayers"—prayers offered by people who never think of praying except when they're in dire need. Isn't this just what's suggested in verse 16? Explain.

**9.** Read Romans 12:1–2. Paul calls us to give our bodies to God as living sacrifices (v. 1). How would that decision actually change the way most of us live?

**10.** How does all that you know about "God's mercy" motivate you to make this "spiritual act of worship" (v. 1)?

**11.** What are some ways in which Christians "conform . . . to the pattern of this world" (v. 2)?

**12.** Paul's command "Be transformed" (v. 2) is both *active* (something we must obey) and *passive* (something done to us by God). How can both be true?

**13.** According to Paul, why should we feel confident rather than fearful about submitting to God's will (vv. 1–2)?

**14.** Take time now to thank God for his mercy and for his good, pleasing, and perfect will. Respond to his mercy by offering yourself to him as a "spiritual act of worship."

## MEMORY VERSE

*Therefore, I urge you, brothers, in view of God's mercy, to offer your bodies as living sacrifices, holy and pleasing to God—this is your spiritual act of worship.*

Romans 12:1

## BETWEEN STUDIES

Comedian and Christian youth speaker Ken Davis has a presentation entitled, "God Wants Your Body." His point is that it's easy to say you're going to give your *life* to Christ—that's nice and vague. But when you talk about giving your *body* to Christ, it becomes a more practical matter. It means that whatever your body does must be honoring to God.

Identify one area of your life that's not yet surrendered to God's will. In light of his mercy, resolve to surrender that area to him this week. Decide, in practical terms (your behavior, way of speaking, use of money, and so on) just what this decision means.

## FOR FURTHER STUDY

Read Matthew 4:1–11 concerning Jesus' temptation by Satan. Identify the ways in which he was tempted. What tool did Jesus use to respond to temptation in each of the three cases in this passage? Study the following passages and consider what kinds of temptation Jesus must have been facing: Matthew 16:21–23; 26:36–56. See Hebrews 2:17–18 for a discussion of the reasons and purposes for Christ's temptation.

# *Leader's Notes*

Leading a Bible discussion—especially for the first time—can make you feel both nervous and excited. If you are nervous, realize that you are in good company. Many biblical leaders, such as Moses, Joshua, and the apostle Paul, felt nervous and inadequate to lead others (see, for example, 1 Corinthians 2:3). Yet God's grace was sufficient for them, just as it will be for you.

Some excitement is also natural. Your leadership is a gift to the others in the group. Keep in mind, however, that other group members also share responsibility for the group. Your role is simply to stimulate discussion by asking questions and encouraging people to respond. The suggestions listed below can help you to be an effective leader.

## PREPARING TO LEAD

1. Ask God to help you understand and apply the passage to your own life. Unless that happens, you will not be prepared to lead others.

2. Carefully work through each question in the study guide. Meditate and reflect on the passage as you formulate your answers.

3. Familiarize yourself with the leader's notes for the study. These will help you understand the purpose of the study and will provide valuable information about the questions in the study.

4. Pray for the various members of the group. Ask God to use these studies to make you better disciples of Jesus Christ.

5. Before the first meeting, make sure each person has a study guide. Encourage them to prepare beforehand for each study.

## LEADING THE STUDY

1. Begin the study on time. If people realize that the study begins on schedule, they will work harder to arrive on time.

2. At the beginning of your first time together, explain that these studies are designed to be discussions, not lectures. Encourage everyone to participate, but realize that some may be hesitant to speak during the first few sessions.

3. Read the introductory paragraph at the beginning of the discussion. This will orient the group to the passage being studied.

4. Read the passage aloud. You may choose to do this yourself, or you might ask for volunteers.

5. The questions in the guide are designed to be used just as they are written. If you wish, you may simply read each one aloud to the group. Or you may prefer to express them in your own words. Unnecessary rewording of the questions, however, is not recommended.

6. Don't be afraid of silence. People in the group may need time to think before responding.

7. Avoid answering your own questions. If necessary, rephrase a question until it is clearly understood. Even an

eager group will quickly become passive and silent if they think the leader will do most of the talking.

8. Encourage more than one answer to each question. Ask, "What do the rest of you think?" or "Anyone else?" until several people have had a chance to respond.

9. Try to be affirming whenever possible. Let people know you appreciate their insights into the passage.

10. Never reject an answer. If it is clearly wrong, ask, "Which verse led you to that conclusion?" Or let the group handle the problem by asking them what they think about the question.

11. Avoid going off on tangents. If people wander off course, gently bring them back to the passage being considered.

12. Conclude your time together with conversational prayer. Ask God to help you apply those things that you learned in the study.

13. End on time. This will be easier if you control the pace of the discussion by not spending too much time on some questions or too little on others.

Many more suggestions and helps are found in the book *Leading Bible Discussions* (InterVarsity Press). Reading it would be well worth your time.

## STUDY 1
### *God's Great Mercy to Us*
*ROMANS 3:9–20; EPHESIANS 2:1–10*

**Purpose:** To realize that God's great mercy to us is the foundation for our showing mercy to others.

**Question 1** Every study begins with an "approach question," which is discussed *before* reading the passage. An approach question is designed to do three things.

First, it helps to break the ice. Because an approach question doesn't require any knowledge of the passage or any special preparation, it can get people talking and can help them to warm up to each other.

Second, an approach question can motivate people to study the passage at hand. At the beginning of the study, people in the group aren't necessarily ready to jump into the world of the Bible. Their minds may be on other things (their kids, a problem at work, an upcoming meeting) that have nothing to do with the study. An approach question can capture their interest and draw them into the discussion by raising important issues related to the study. The question becomes a bridge between their personal lives and the answers found in Scripture.

Third, a good approach question can reveal where people's thoughts or feelings need to be transformed by Scripture. That is why it is important to ask the approach question *before* reading the passage. The passage might inhibit the spontaneous, honest answers people might have given, because they feel compelled to give biblical answers. The approach question allows them to compare their personal thoughts and feelings with what they later discover in Scripture.

In this first question, don't push your group toward an emotional "confession time" of deep sin. It is sufficient that they discuss minor weaknesses they can laugh about. The purpose of the question, of course, is to set the stage for discussing spiritual life and death. All of us are guilty of transgressions that bring spiritual death.

**Question 4** Common sins of the tongue include gossip, backbiting, angry words, intentionally hurting someone's feelings, bragging, building yourself up at someone else's expense, and so on.

**Question 7** If your group has trouble with this question, encourage them to think about the differences between the

Garden of Eden before the Fall (free access to God, lack of self-consciousness, easier relationships between people) and after the Fall, when spiritual death entered the world. The spiritually dead are, of course, cut off from God (see Ps. 66:18, for instance). Spiritually dead people are antagonistic toward God, they reject him (Rom. 1:18–23), and they are incapable of understanding spiritual things (1 Cor. 1:18; 2:14). In essence, there is an entire area of reality that the unsaved are, indeed, "dead" to. They have been described as: "A living corpse: without the gracious presence of God's Spirit in the soul, and so unable to think, will, or do aught that is holy" (From Jamieson, Fausset, and Brown, *Commentary on the Whole Bible* [Grand Rapids, Mich.: Zondervan Publishing House, 1961], p. 1282).

**Question 8** In the second part of this question, encourage the group to think of some of the "theological" manifestations of God's love, mercy, grace, and kindness. These include, for example, our salvation and the gift of the Holy Spirit. Think, too, of the day-to-day manifestations, such as the privilege of prayer and God's kindness in responding to those prayers, the comfort of Christian friends, hope, the fruit of the Spirit, and so on.

**Questions 9–10** Just as we were once dead to God and to the entire spiritual realm of life, now, through God's mercy, we have been made alive to that spiritual realm, in this life and the life to come.

Other aspects of our spiritual life include the following:

- A new and different future (2 Cor. 5:17)
- A more vitalized and fruitful physical life (Rom. 8:11; 7:4)
- Eternal life (2 Cor. 5:4; John 3:15–36)
- Being identified with Christ rather than Adam
- Being set free from the slavery to sin (Rom. 6:6–7)
- Belonging to a new family—the family (body) of Christ (1 Cor. 12:13; Mark 3:33–34)

## STUDY 2
# *Being Merciful to Others*
*LUKE 6:32–36; MATTHEW 5:43–6:4*

**Purpose:** To explore the implications of the extreme mercy Christ preached in the Sermon on the Mount and to consider the differences between that extreme mercy and the dominant ethics of our society.

**Question 2** The purpose of this question is to show that the standards Christ holds up for godly people are far higher than the world deems prudent—so high as to seem foolish to those this passage refers to as "sinners." Even sinners love their friends; godly people should love their *enemies.* Even sinners do good to their friends; godly people should do good to their enemies. Even sinners lend to those who will repay them; godly people should lend to those who won't or can't repay. Will we be rewarded by those enemies? Not likely—but our reward will be great nevertheless.

Matthew Henry tells us that "we must not only *love our ene-mies,* and bear a good will to them, but we must *do good* to them. We must study to make it appear, by positive acts, that we bear them no malice, nor seek revenge. . . . This should strongly engage us to be merciful to our brethren, not only that God is so to others, but that he is so to us, though we have been, and are, evil and unthankful; it is of his mercies that we are not consumed" (*Matthew Henry's Commentary in One Volume* [Grand Rapids, Mich.: Zondervan Publishing House, 1961], pp. 1432–33).

**Question 3** Don't press group members to respond to this question if they seem uneasy with it. Let those contribute who seem willing to, and then move on. Many people, rightly or wrongly, have poor memories of childhood and feel that they were treated kindly by no one. Don't take the chance of angering or depressing anyone in your group over this question, and thereby decreasing the effectiveness of the study for them.

**Question 4** This question is designed to spur discussion about the practical outworking of Jesus' ethic for mercy in daily life. Encourage your group to be as specific and as practical as possible in their answers. Don't be afraid to devote a significant percentage of your group time to this question. It's easy to be committed to mercy as an abstract principle, but when we see how alien it is to the way we live our everyday lives, we suddenly become aware of the cost of mercy.

Your group will probably want to engage in "Yeah buts," raising the practical objections to this ethic of mercy: "But if I really try that at work, my boss will walk all over me." Allow a few responses of that type to make it clear that there is a cost associated with this ethic. But try not to let the conversation degenerate into head-shaking about the impracticality of living mercifully. Rather, keep your group busy describing how they can live by the ethic of mercy in their daily life.

**Question 5** His leaving heaven to become a man and die on the cross for undeserving sinners is the prime example (Matt. 27:11–66). Others include the following:

- Jesus' expression of compassion toward unresponsive Judaism (Matt. 23:37)
- his reinstatement of Peter to a place of importance as a disciple after Peter denied him (John 21:15–18)
- Jesus' healing the ear of the servant who had come with those who wanted to arrest him (Luke 22:49–51)
- his forgiveness and protection of the woman taken in adultery (John 8:1–11)

We might also include any of the miracles, since we are all undeserving of his intercession for us (see, for example, Luke 5:1–11 and 6:17–19; Mark 1:23–26, 34 and 3:1–5; Matt. 8:1–4, 16–17; 9:1–8, 27–31; 14:15–21).

**Question 7** All of us have petty squabbles or personality conflicts at work, home, or even at church—people who don't approve of the way we're doing things and who oppose us, drag their feet, and talk behind our backs. These are our "enemies" for the purposes of this passage. And even our friends can sometimes be our "enemies" if they oppose us or become estranged from us for a period of time.

**Question 8** Having a personal "accountability partner"—a Christian friend close enough and trusted enough to hold you accountable when you're wrong or when you fall—is one way. A daily evaluation time is another effective way, especially if you ask God to let you know during those times when your motives have not been proper.

## STUDY 3
## *Models of Mercy*
*MARK 10:46–52; LUKE 10:25–37*

**Purpose:** To find in the teachings and in the personal actions of Jesus models for our own exercise of mercy.

**Question 4** Bartimaeus didn't immediately request his sight—he requested mercy: "Have mercy on me!" Others healed by Jesus began with the same request. They saw more clearly than we do today that God's response to our prayers is, indeed, a merciful act toward a needy, undeserving person. Even when we need healing, we don't like to think of ourselves in need of mercy. Only after Jesus had responded to his request for mercy did the blind man ask for healing of his sight.

**Question 5** It is significant that the blind man's immediate response was to begin following Jesus. (This may not mean, however, that Bartimaeus became a disciple of Jesus. As Walter W. Wessel points out: "Mark's statement that the blind man followed Jesus is best taken to mean . . . that the man joined the crowd going up to the feast" (*Mark,* The Expositor's

Bible Commentary [Grand Rapids, Mich.: Zondervan Publishing House, 1984], p. 722). Still, the symbolic meaning of the statement is significant. An act of mercy toward an undeserving person can become an act of evangelism, encouraging the recipient to follow the One who made that act possible. People in need often receive the message of the gospel much more readily when their bodily needs have been met.

**Question 6** They were probably concerned for their own safety. It could have been a trap; the robbers who injured the man could have been hiding nearby, waiting for someone else. The priest and the Levite may also have been reluctant to offer help because of the personal cost involved, not only of money but of time and inconvenience. This consideration doesn't seem to have bothered the Samaritan, since he was generous with all three.

**Question 7** The priest and the Levite were certainly guilty of a sin of omission in not stopping to help their countryman. They knew enough about the law to realize that they were expected to stop and offer aid even to fallen donkeys and enemies (see Deut. 22:4, Exod. 23:4, and Isa. 58:7). They may even have been returning home from performing their priestly duties! Yet they still passed by the bleeding, injured man.

**Question 9** Encourage the group to identify racial, religious, occupational, or cultural groups that are typically mistrusted or disliked in your community. Don't allow the discussion to degenerate into a complaint session about these groups. Identify them, identify the reasons for that prejudice, and then move on. This discussion can destroy group harmony if members of unpopular groups are present, so handle this discussion carefully.

**Question 10** Don't let your group get away with a simple yes or no answer to this question. They may be unwilling to acknowledge that they'd simply pass by someone in need, especially in a discussion of the good Samaritan. Think up specific situations—someone with a flat tire or out of gas, someone in need of medical help, someone being mugged or robbed, someone whose house has burned down and has nowhere to sleep. Discuss the inconsistency of being willing to *accept* help from a particular group but not being willing to *offer* it.

## STUDY 4
### *Getting What You Give*
MATTHEW 5:7; 18:21–35

**Purpose:** To realize that, whether we like it or not, God clearly states in the Bible that we must show mercy if we want to be shown mercy.

**Question 1** The question of fairness may seem somewhat irrelevant to this study, but this initial discussion is necessary to set up the final question, which *is* relevant. Your group will probably define fairness in the sense of reciprocity, almost the Golden Rule: You should treat other people the way you want to be treated, or as they treat you. Or the group may define fairness in the sense of equality: Everybody should be treated equally. In the final question, we'll see that God's definition is broader.

**Question 2** It stands to reason that others will *tend* to treat us as we treat them—although we all know that some people will treat us unkindly or unfairly no matter what we do. It is their choice to make. But as D. A. Carson points out, "The reward is not mercy shown by others but by God" (*Matthew,* The Expositor's Bible Commentary [Grand Rapids, Mich.: Zondervan, 1984], p. 134).

**Question 3** We don't want to believe that we will not be treated mercifully if we don't treat others mercifully, but this verse implies that there is a relationship between the two (and Matt. 6:14–15 reinforces that implication, as well as the passage from Matt. 18 we'll examine next). Don't spend a great deal of time on this question, since the discussion of Matthew

18 will help clarify the issue, but do allow your group to explore the implications of this perplexing and troubling truth. D. A. Carson reassures us, "This does not mean that our mercy is the causal ground of God's mercy but its occasional ground" (*Matthew,* p. 134).

**Question 4** Peter's question was probably motivated by frustration or anger. He may have been feeling unforgiving toward the other disciples—possibly because of a disagreement among them in the early verses of this chapter about who was the greatest in the kingdom of heaven. If that's true, he certainly didn't want to hear that we need to offer virtually limitless forgiveness to our brothers and sisters.

**Question 5** "As long as it shall be needed and sought, you are never to come to the point of refusing forgiveness sincerely asked" (Jamieson, Fausset and Brown, p. 935). Compare Luke 17:3–4.

**Question 6** In this country, pursuing a debtor to the limits of the law would probably include a civil suit that would claim all of his possessions as well as much of his earnings for several years. That judgment would clearly have a negative effect not only on your debtor but on his family as well.

**Questions 7–8** Allow your group to explore the extent of this debt and to imagine their relief at its removal. But keep in mind that the purpose of these two questions isn't to plumb the depths of God's forgiveness, but rather to demonstrate how vindictive and ungrateful the wicked servant was, who having been forgiven such a great debt, refused to forgive a much smaller one.

**Question 9** The idea behind "debtor's prison" was that in order to get out of prison a debtor would borrow money from friends and family to pay his debts. So it was, in theory, possible to throw someone into prison to recover a bad debt. But the wicked servant's extreme actions (choking the debtor) and his insistence on prison even though the debtor agreed to pay the debt indicate that the servant was not only unmerciful, but he was also vindictive. He apparently wanted revenge more than repayment of his money.

The wicked servant's action was also questionable legally, especially considering that the unfortunate debtor owed the wicked servant only about a hundred denarii. D. A. Carson tells us that "even an inexpensive slave sold for five hundred denarii, and it was illegal to sell a man for a sum greater than his debt" (*Matthew,* p. 407).

Yet the primary thrust of Jesus' parable is an argument from the greater to the lesser: Because the servant had been forgiven such an enormous debt, how much more should he have forgiven the relatively small debt that was owed to him?

**Question 10** The purpose of this discussion is not merely to understand the great debt we have been forgiven, but to understand how important it is for us, having received that forgiveness, to exercise the same mercy and forgiveness toward others who've sinned against us in comparatively insignificant ways.

Don't let your group miss the theologically difficult but inescapable point in verses 32–35: God will withhold his mercy from us if we do not exercise mercy toward others. D. A. Carson writes that "Jesus sees no incongruity in the actions of a heavenly Father who forgives so bountifully and punishes so ruthlessly, and neither should we. Indeed, it is precisely because he is a God of such compassion and mercy that he cannot possibly accept as his those devoid of compassion and mercy. This is not to say that the king's compassion can be earned: far from it, the servant is granted freedom only by virtue of the king's forgiveness. As in 6:12, 14–15, those who are forgiven must forgive, lest they show themselves incapable of receiving forgiveness" (*Matthew,* p. 407).

**Question 11** The "fairness" issue should now be clear to your group: Our exercise of mercy and forgiveness toward others isn't based on how they treat us, nor is it based on some notion of equality; it is based on how God has already treated us. We see clearly that it was unfair of the wicked servant to demand immediate payment from his debtor, because God had already forgiven the wicked servant's debt. The Christian view of fairness is based less on equality and reciprocity than it is on gratitude for the wonderful gifts of God and a desire to let his love and mercy shine through us. It is a "three-way" fairness, not a "two-way" fairness, born of a desire to be found worthy of God's great gifts.

## STUDY 5
## *Mercy, Not Sacrifice*
*MICAH 6:6–8; MATTHEW 12:1–13; 23:23*

**Purpose:** To realize that God's ultimate concern and desire is not that we legalistically follow certain rules but that we show compassion, mercy, and justice to those in need.

**Question 2** Ironically, the well-churched may have a more difficult time with this question than the new Christians in your group. Those of us who've been raised in the church have been conditioned to elevate to "ten-commandment" status such practices as never missing a Sunday in church, attending evening and midweek services, tithing, serving on church committees and boards, listening to only Christian music, dressing and grooming ourselves according to some vague "evangelical" guideline, having daily devotions, and so on. But the point is that even though these things may be good, they are no proof of spirituality. You don't have to be a Christian to do these things, and many Christians do them with a bitter or proud or self-righteous spirit.

**Question 3** Even though these things may be good in themselves (as the Old Testament sacrifices were), they don't *necessarily* indicate the condition of the heart. Yet when we studiously observe such religious practices and ignore compassion, justice, and mercy, we become guilty of the sin of the Pharisees.

**Question 4** It's hard to see what's really going on inside a person's heart, and such things as mercy and justice aren't easily measured. So we tend to encourage those things that *are* easily measured: church attendance, tithing, manner of dress, and so on. We evaluate each other's spiritual condition on the basis of the least reliable indicators, rather than looking for each other's progress in the things God loves.

**Question 5** If our relationship with God is weak, then our efforts at exercising justice and mercy toward others will be hamstrung. And if we refuse to exercise justice and mercy toward others—evidence of a prideful spirit—we'll be unable to relate humbly with the God whom we are clearly disobeying.

**Question 6** A person can *show* mercy grudgingly, with regrets. The person who *loves* mercy will exercise it with enthusiasm. The person who loves mercy will also encourage it in others, will defend it against its detractors, and will campaign for mercy when it is in short supply.

**Question 7** Justice has its negative side as well as its positive. It can demand equal treatment for all and fairness for all, but it can also demand the full, unflinching imposition of all legally prescribed penalties when an infraction occurs. Mercy, on the other hand, begs for forgiveness and grace instead of punishment.

Two thoughts help bring balance. First, it's not justice if you repeatedly exercise mercy toward one person or group and harsh justice toward another person or group. That is prejudice or favoritism. Express both justice and mercy toward all. Second, there are times when it is not a mercy to deny someone the full weight of law. For instance, it's unwise to ask to have a penalty removed from someone who has broken a law, because you're increasing the likelihood that the individual will break the law again—perhaps with more serious consequences.

**Question 9** D. A. Carson explains that "the relevance of this quotation from the 'latter prophets' depends on the Pharisees' attitude to the law being as worthy of condemnation as the attitude of those who relied superficially and hypocritically on mere ritual in Hosea's day. Jesus claims, in effect, that the Pharisees had not really grasped the significance of the law, and this was demonstrated by their Halakah" (*Matthew*, p. 282).

*Halakah* refers to the body of Jewish law and tradition in its entirety: biblical law, oral traditions and laws transcribed in the Talmud, and any more recent codes (and the Pharisees had many) added to clarify disputes or codify later precepts. Jesus seems to be directing his comment toward the legalistic mindset of the Pharisees that caused them to question his act of mercy on a point of law. Having learned to live entirely by the book, they are unable to accept a spontaneous act of mercy and generosity. In their lives, legality supersedes goodness.

**Question 10** The sheep, of course, has monetary value. And since the sheep belongs to the Pharisees, saving it could essentially be an act of self-interest—protecting their investment—whereas healing the man with the withered arm would be an act of compassion, unrelated to their own interest. But the purpose of Jesus' question is not so much to compare the relative worth of the sheep and the man as it is to suggest a deeper question: "Was the Sabbath a day for maleficent activity—like their evil intentions in questioning him—or for beneficent action, like the healing about to be done?" (D. A. Carson, *Matthew*, p. 284). Stung by the realization of the truth Jesus had spoken, their guilty consciences may have prompted their desire to kill him.

**Question 12** The clear scriptural principle is this: "The Lord does not look at the things we look at. We look at the outward appearance, but the Lord looks at the heart" (1 Sam. 16:7). In all our actions, our motive should not be a desire to adhere to a strict standard of behavior, as the Pharisees did, nor a desire to be "seen of men" to be righteous. Rather, our motive should be a deep commitment to justice, mercy, love, and the other "weightier matters of the law."

## STUDY 6
## *Responding to God's Mercy*
*HEBREWS 4:14–16; ROMANS 12:1–2*

**Purpose:** To emphasize God's readiness to extend mercy to us, and to explore the proper response on our part to that outpouring of God's mercy.

**Question 1** It will take some imagination on your group members' parts to realize how they've stereotyped God, and some of them may resist participating in this question. Encourage them to at least try, because the point of some of the later questions will be far stronger for them if they have their own image of God in mind. (If people don't feel comfortable with the images in the list, suggest that they come up with their own.)

**Question 2** God is far more forgiving and full of grace and mercy and acceptance than we realize. Few of us truly believe that Christ is able to "sympathize with our weaknesses" (v. 15); instead, we imagine his condemnation and disgust when we're tempted or when we sin. Few, if any, of your group members will characterize God as more merciful and benevolent than this passage in Hebrews describes him; instead, they'll see him as more vindictive and legalistic.

**Question 3** See the "For Further Study" section for some passages relating to Jesus' temptations.

Leon Morris writes that "though Jesus did not sin, we must not infer that life was easy for him. His sinlessness was, at least in part, an earned sinlessness as he gained victory after victory in the constant battle with temptation that life in this world entails. Many have pointed out that the Sinless One knows the force of temptation in a way that we who sin do not. We give in before the temptation has fully spent itself; only he who does not yield knows its full force" (*Hebrews,* The Expositor's Bible Commentary [Grand Rapids, Mich.: Zondervan, 1981], p. 46).

**Question 4** Encourage your group to be as practical as possible in their response to this question, suggesting specific actions and strategies for daily holding "firmly to the faith we profess" and approaching "the throne of grace with confidence."

**Question 5** As your group composes their prayer for mercy and grace, encourage them to include the primary elements of prayer: praise, thanksgiving, confession, and petition.

**Question 6** The most obvious expressions of God's mercy, of course, are the theological ones: our salvation itself and the gift of the Holy Spirit. But encourage your group to do some real brainstorming here about how we experience God's mercy daily. We experience it at every level: physical, emotional, spiritual, and social. Even though God often allows us to experience trials in those areas, he also gives us the grace and strength and resources to withstand them. And there is much that he spares us.

**Question 8** The problem with "foxhole prayers" is that they're often spoken by people who never pray otherwise. If our prayer life is regular and healthy, we have the basis in our relationship to God to come to him with our desperate needs—as indeed he expects us to, according to this verse. If our prayer life is not healthy, then we're like the child who only speaks to his parents when he wants to ask them for something.

**Question 9** It might be helpful to divide your group's discussion of this question into the physical, social, intellectual, and emotional implications of the decision. How might our inter-action with other people change? How might our use of our bodies change (or the way we treat our bodies) now that they're no longer our own? How might our use of our minds (our reading matter, our study habits, our use of media, and our choice of entertainment) change? Is there anything in our expression of emotions or the way in which we're controlled by our moods that needs to change, or that is likely to change?

**Question 11** Everett F. Harrison writes that "the believer has been delivered from this present evil age (Gal 1:4), which has Satan for its god (2 Cor 4:4). He lives by the powers of the age to come (Heb 6:5), but his heavenly calling includes resi-dence in this world, among sinful men, where he is to show forth the praises of him who called him out of darkness into God's marvelous light. He is in the world for witness, but not for conformity to that which is a passing phenomenon (1 Cor 7:31)" (*Romans,* The Expositor's Bible Commentary [Grand Rapids, Mich.: Zondervan, 1976], p. 128).

Your group should have no trouble thinking of ways in which they're tempted to conform not to God's will but rather to worldly standards. If they balk, here are a few possibilities that might get them started: materialism, greed, selfish ambition to succeed even at the expense of others, unhealthy competi-tion, lust, sensuality, self-centeredness, gluttony, laziness, and substance abuse.

**Question 13** Matthew Henry comments that "God is a merci-ful God, therefore let us present our bodies to him; he will be sure to use them kindly. We receive from him every day the fruits of his mercy, particularly mercy to our bodies: he made them, he maintains them, he bought them. The greatest mercy of all is that Christ hath made not his body only, but his soul, an offering for sin. Let us render ourselves as an acknowledg-ment of all these favours—all we are, all we have, all we can do; and, after all, it is but very poor returns" (*Matthew Henry's Commentary,* p. 1784).

# Notes

# Notes